STEP-BY-STEP

Barbecues

STEP-BY-STEP

Barbecues

CARA HOBDAY

This edition printed in 1995 for:
Shooting Star Press Inc
230 Fifth Avenue – Suite 1212
New York, NY 10001

Shooting Star Press books are available at special discounts for bulk purchases for sales promotions,
premiums, fund-raising, or educational use. Special edition or book excerpts can also be created to
specification. For details contact: Special Sales Director, Shooting Star Press Inc.,
230 Fifth Avenue, Suite 1212, New York, NY 10001

ISBN 1-57335-110-5

Produced by Haldane Mason, London

Printed in Italy

Acknowledgements:
Art Direction: Ron Samuels
Editor: Joanna Swinnerton
Series Design: Pedro & Frances Prá-Lopez/Kingfisher Design
Page Design: Somewhere Creative
Photography: Iain Bagwell
Stylist: Rachel Jukes
Home Economist: Cara Hobday

Photographs on pages 6, 20, 34, 48 & 62 are reproduced by permission of
ZEFA Picture Library (UK) Ltd.

The photographer would like to thank Ceramica Blue and Webber Barbecues
for the use of props.

Note:
*Unless otherwise stated, milk is assumed to be full-fat, eggs are AA extra large and pepper is
freshly ground black pepper.*

Contents

❧

CHAPTER ONE

Poultry

Thanks to modern farming methods, chicken is no longer just chicken. There are free-range, corn-fed, ready-basted, and organic birds, and much of this applies to other poultry, such as turkey, duck, and goose. When you go shopping, bear in mind what the poultry is to be used for. If you are going to marinate it heavily, or cover it in Cajun spices, then go for ordinary chicken pieces. In a subtle marinade, such as the one used for Mediterranean Grilled Chicken, the flavor of the chicken will contribute to the dish, so it may be worth buying a free-range or corn-fed bird. If you plan to cook a dish with sauce, where the poultry is simply grilled, such as Tasmanian Duck, it is worth buying the best you can afford.

It is possible to barbecue turkey, but steps must be taken to insure the meat does not dry out. Start with meat of even thickness, or hammer your meat to an even thickness if it is boneless. Then you could marinate it in an oil-based mix, which will help a little, and baste often during cooking. The meat will retain moisture if cooked in a kettle barbecue with the lid on, over a small can of water above the coals.

Young game birds and tender cuts of game meat, such as loin or fillet of venison, or pieces of rabbit, are also delicious barbecued.

Opposite: *The beauty of barbecues is being able to set them up almost anywhere for an unforgettable feast.*

STEP 2

STEP 3

STEP 5

STEP 6

TANDOORI CHICKEN

A tandoor oven is a huge urn sunk in the ground. Charcoal is burned in the bottom, and cooking begins after about 2 hours when only the white-hot embers remain and the oven is searing hot. The meat is threaded on skewers, and basted often during the short cooking time.

SERVES 6

3 dried red chilies
2 tbsp coriander seed
2 tsp turmeric
2 tsp garam masala
4 garlic cloves, crushed
1/2 onion, chopped
1-in. piece gingerroot, peeled and grated
2 tbsp lime juice
1 tsp salt
1/2 cup natural yogurt
1 tbsp oil
1 × 4-pound chicken, cut into 6 pieces

TO SERVE:
Kachumber (see page 76)
Raita (see page 76)

1 Grind together the chilies, coriander seed, turmeric, garam masala, garlic, onion, gingerroot, lime juice and salt in a pestle and mortar or grinder.

2 Put a skillet over a low heat, and add the spice paste. Stir until fragrant, about 2 minutes. Transfer to a shallow non-porous bowl.

3 Add the yogurt and oil, and mix well to combine.

4 Remove the skin from the chicken pieces, and make 3 slashes in the flesh of each piece. Add the chicken to the dish, and make sure that the pieces are coated completely in the marinade. Cover and chill for at least 4 hours. Remove from the refrigerator, and leave, covered, at room temperature for 30 minutes.

5 Wrap the chicken pieces in foil.

6 Cook the chicken pieces over a very hot barbecue for about 15 minutes, turning once. Remove the foil, with the aid of a pair of tongs, and brown the chicken on the barbecue for 5 minutes. Serve with the raita and/or kachumber.

SEALING MEAT

When meat or poultry is cooked over a very hot barbecue, the heat immediately seals in all the juices, leaving the flesh succulent. For this reason you must make sure that the coals are hot enough before starting to grill.

STEP 1

STEP 2

STEP 4

STEP 5

FILIPINO CHICKEN

This recipe is one of a large repertoire borrowed from a Filipino friend. Tomato ketchup is a very popular ingredient in Asian dishes, as it has a zingy sweet-sour flavor.

SERVES 4

1 can lemonade or lime-and-lemonade
2 tbsp gin
4 tbsp tomato ketchup
2 tsp garlic salt
2 tsp Worcestershire sauce
4 chicken breast fillets
salt and pepper

TO SERVE:
thread egg noodles
1 green chili, finely chopped
2 scallions, sliced

1 Combine the lemonade or lime-and-lemonade, gin, tomato ketchup, garlic salt, Worcestershire sauce and seasoning in a large non-porous dish.

2 Put the chicken breast fillets into the dish, and make sure that the marinade covers them completely.

3 Let marinate in the refrigerator for 2 hours. Remove and leave, covered, at room temperature for 30 minutes.

4 Place the chicken over a medium barbecue, and cook for 20 minutes.

5 Turn the chicken once, halfway through the cooking time.

6 Remove from the barbecue, and let rest for 3–4 minutes before serving.

7 Serve with egg noodles, tossed with a little green chili and scallions.

PERFECT CHICKEN

Cooking the meat on the bone after it has reached room temperature means that it cooks in a shorter time, which insures that the meat remains moist right through to the bone.

STEP 1

STEP 2

STEP 4

STEP 4

MEDITERRANEAN GRILLED CHICKEN

Chargrilling and barbecuing are popular methods of cooking on the Mediterranean. This recipe uses ingredients found in the Languedoc area of France, where cooking over hot embers is a way of life.

SERVES 4

4 tbsp natural yogurt
3 tbsp sun-dried tomato paste
1 tbsp olive oil
¼ cup fresh basil leaves, lightly crushed
2 garlic cloves, roughly chopped
4 chicken quarters

1 Combine the yogurt, tomato paste, olive oil, basil leaves and garlic in a small bowl and stir well to mix.

2 Put the marinade into a bowl large enough to hold the chicken quarters in a single layer. Add the chicken quarters. Make sure that the chicken pieces are thoroughly coated in the marinade by turning them in it, and spooning the marinade over them.

3 Let marinate in the refrigerator for 2 hours. Remove and leave, covered, at room temperature for 30 minutes.

4 Place the chicken over a preheated medium barbecue, and cook for 30–40 minutes, turning frequently. Test for readiness by piercing the flesh at the thickest part – usually at the top of the drumstick. If the juices that run out are clear, it is cooked through, but cook for 10 minutes longer if the juices have blood in them.

5 Serve hot with a green salad. It is also delicious eaten cold.

VARIATION

For a marinade with a zingy flavor combine 2 garlic cloves, coarsely chopped, the juice of 2 lemons and 3 tbsp olive oil, and cook in the same way.

Whether you cook the chicken with the skin on or off is up to you. The chicken will be higher in fat if the skin is left on, but many people like the rich taste and a crispy skin, especially when it is blackened by the barbecue.

TASMANIAN DUCK

*Some of the best cherries in the world are grown in Tasmania,
hence the title for this recipe, though dried cherries from any country
can be used.*

STEP 1

SERVES 4

4 duck breasts
¹/₂ cup dried cherries
¹/₂ cup water
4 tbsp lemon juice
2 large leeks, quartered, or 8 baby leeks
2 tbsp olive oil
2 tbsp balsamic vinegar
2 tbsp port
2 tsp pink peppercorns

1 Make 3 slashes in the fat of the duck breasts in one direction, and 3 in the other.

2 Put the dried cherries, water and lemon juice into a small saucepan. Bring to a boil. Remove from the heat, and let cool.

3 Turn a large foil tray upside-down, and make several holes in the bottom with a skewer. Put it over a hot barbecue.

4 Put the duck into the tray. Cover with foil, and cook for 20 minutes.

5 Brush the leeks with oil, and cook on the open barbecue for 5–7 minutes, turning constantly.

6 Remove the duck from the tray, and cook on the open barbecue for 5 minutes, skin-side down, while you make the sauce.

7 Stir the balsamic vinegar into the cooking sauces in the tray, scraping any bits from the bottom. Add to the cherries in the saucepan. Return to the heat – either the stove top or barbecue – and stir in the port and pink peppercorns. Bring to a boil, and cook for 5 minutes, until the sauce has thickened slightly.

8 Serve the duck piping hot. Pour over the cherries and sauce, and accompany with the leeks.

STEP 3

STEP 4

FOIL TRAYS

It is useful to keep some foil trays on hand. The rectangular shape is the most convenient for reheating, freezing and protecting delicate food on the barbecue.

STEP 7

15

STEP 1

STEP 2

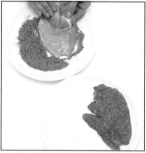

STEP 4

STEP 6

BLACKENED CHICKEN WITH GUACAMOLE

French Cajun cooking has its roots in earthy, strong flavors, and uses plenty of spice. This easy recipe includes a typical Cajun spice mix.

SERVES 4

4 skinless, boned chicken breasts
¼ cup butter, melted

SPICE MIX:
1 tsp salt
1 tbsp sweet paprika
1 tsp dried onion granules
1 tsp dried garlic granules
1 tsp dried thyme
1 tsp cayenne
½ tsp cracked black pepper
½ tsp dried oregano

GUACAMOLE:
1 avocado
1 tbsp lemon juice
2 tbsp sour cream
½ red onion, chopped and rinsed
1 garlic clove, halved

1 Put each chicken breast between 2 pieces of plastic wrap and pound with a mallet or rolling pin until it is an even thickness. It will be about ½ in. thick.

2 Brush each chicken breast all over with the melted butter. Set aside.

3 Combine the spice mix ingredients in a shallow bowl.

4 Coat the chicken breasts with the spice mix, insuring that they are covered completely. Set aside.

5 Mash the avocado thoroughly with the lemon juice in a small bowl. Stir in the sour cream and red onion.

6 Wipe the garlic clove around the guacamole serving dish, pressing hard. Spoon in the guacamole.

7 Place the chicken breasts over the hottest part of a very hot barbecue, and cook for 8–10 minutes, turning once.

8 Slice the breasts into thick pieces, and serve immediately with the guacamole.

VARIATION

To enjoy this recipe out of the barbecue season, the chicken may also be cooked in a dry pan. Heat a heavy-based skillet until it is searing hot, and cook the chicken for about 4 minutes on each side.

STEP 2

STEP 3

STEP 4

STEP 6

CHARGRILLED CHICKEN SALAD

This is a quick dish to serve while your hungry guests are waiting for the main event. If the bread is bent in half, the chicken salad can be put in the middle, and eaten as finger food – remember to provide napkins!

SERVES 4

2 chicken breasts
1 red onion, peeled
oil for brushing
1 avocado, peeled and pitted
1 tbsp lemon juice
$^1/_2$ cup mayonnaise
$^1/_4$ tsp chili powder
$^1/_2$ tsp pepper
$^1/_4$ tsp salt
4 tomatoes, quartered
$^1/_2$ loaf sun-dried tomato-flavored focaccia
    bread

1 Cut the chicken breasts into $^1/_2$ in. strips.

2 Cut the red onion into 8 pieces, held together at the root. Rinse and brush them with oil.

3 Purée or mash the avocado and lemon juice together. Whisk in the mayonnaise. Add in the chili powder, pepper and salt.

4 Put the chicken and onion over a hot barbecue, and grill for 3–4 minutes on each side.

5 Mix the chicken, onion, tomato and avocado together.

6 Cut the bread in half twice, so that you have quarter-circle-shaped pieces, then in half horizontally. Toast on the hot barbecue for about 2 minutes on each side.

7 Spoon the chicken mixture on top of the toasts, and serve with a green salad.

PITTING AVOCADOS

Hold the avocado in one hand, and, using a vegetable knife, cut around the middle, so that you are left with two symmetrical halves. Put one half on a dishcloth in one hand, and rap the vegetable knife sharply across the avocado pit. The knife will embed itself and it will be simple to lift the pit out with the knife. If you are puréeing the avocado, spoon out the flesh; otherwise peel off the skin carefully.

CHAPTER TWO

Fish & Seafood

Barbecuing is an excellent way, perhaps the best way, to cook fish. As it does not need to cook for long, it retains a lot of flavor, especially if it is wrapped while cooking. When you buy fish, it should be prepared and ready to cook, needing only a few flavorings. Octopus and squid are the exceptions; usually they have to be marinated before cooking to tenderize the flesh. Larger fish, such as swordfish, shark, and tuna, can be cooked in much the same way as chicken or steak. They absorb the flavor of a marinade very well, although the flavor of the fish is still strong enough to come through.

Slightly more delicate fish, such as trout, carp, perch, and turbot, should be wrapped or placed on a bed of herbs, grape leaves, or lemon slices to protect them from the fiercest heat. The smallest fish and fillets, such as sole, cod, herring, mackerel, sardine, and small trout, should be cooked quickly and basted often. A fish rack is useful for keeping the smaller fish in shape.

Shellfish are delicious barbecued. Clams, scallops, and mussels can be barbecued in their shells. Large shrimp can be cooked directly on the grid; small ones should be skewered. And for a special occasion, even lobster can be halved and cooked over a fierce heat.

Opposite: *Fish is easy and delicious to barbecue – and if you can cook it straight from the sea, it will make a truly memorable meal.*

STEP 1

STEP 2

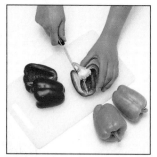

STEP 3

STEP 4

CHARGRILLED TUNA WITH ROASTED BELL PEPPERS

Fresh tuna will be either a small bonito fish, or steaks from a skipjack.
The more delicately flavored fish have a paler flesh.

SERVES 4

4 tuna steaks, about 8 ounces each
3 tbsp lemon juice
4 cups water
6 tbsp olive oil
2 orange bell peppers
2 red bell peppers
12 black olives
1 tsp balsamic vinegar
salt and pepper

1 Put the tuna steaks into a bowl with the lemon juice and water. Leave for 15 minutes.

2 Drain and brush the steaks all over with olive oil, and season well.

3 Halve, core and deseed the bell peppers. Put them over a hot barbecue, and cook for 12 minutes until they are charred all over. Put them into a plastic bag, and close it.

4 Meanwhile, cook the tuna over a hot barbecue for 12–15 minutes, turning once.

5 When the bell peppers are cool enough to handle, peel them, and cut each piece into 4 strips. Toss them with the remaining olive oil, olives and balsamic vinegar.

6 Serve the tuna steaks piping hot, with the roasted bell pepper salad.

PEELING BELL PEPPERS

Red, orange and yellow bell peppers can also be peeled by cooking them in a hot oven for 30 minutes, turning them frequently, or roasting them straight over a naked gas flame, again turning them frequently. In either method, deseed the peppers after peeling.

STEP 1

STEP 2

STEP 3

STEP 5

SALMON FILLET ON A BED OF HERBS

This is a great party dish, as the salmon is cooked in one piece. Even though it is placed on a stack of herbs, it manages to keep a smoky, barbecued flavor.

SERVES 4

¹/₂ large bunch dried thyme
5 fresh rosemary branches, 6–8 inches long
8 bay leaves
2-pound salmon fillet
1 bulb fennel, cut into 8 pieces
2 tbsp lemon juice
2 tbsp olive oil

1 Make a base on a hot barbecue with the dried thyme, rosemary branches, and bay leaves, overlapping them to cover a slightly bigger area than the salmon.

2 Place the salmon on top of the herbs.

3 Arrange the fennel around the edge of the fish.

4 Combine the lemon juice and oil and brush the salmon with it.

5 Cover loosely with a piece of foil, to keep the fish moist.

6 Cook for about 20–30 minutes, basting frequently with the lemon juice mixture.

7 Remove the salmon from the barbecue, cut it into slices, and serve with the fennel.

PARTY DISH

The whole salmon fillet looks very impressive when it is being barbecued on a pile of green herbs, and makes a very effective party piece. Use whatever combination of herbs you may have to hand – but avoid the stronger tasting herbs that are unsuitable for fish, such as sage and marjoram.

While the salmon is cooking, keep your guests' appetites keen with some miniature corn-on-the-cob or another light first course, such as toasted pocket bread and some yogurt-based dips.

Serve the salmon with fresh bread and a crunchy green salad, which will enhance rather than overpower the subtle flavor of the fish.

If you find that a whole 2-pound fillet is difficult to get hold of, you can use a 2-pound piece of salmon "steak" split in half. Place the pieces on the grill close together, so that the fish does not dry out as it cooks. This salmon is also very good cold, served with a herb-flavored mayonnaise.

STEP 2

STEP 3

STEP 4

STEP 5

SCALLOP SKEWERS

As the scallops are marinated, it is not essential that they are fresh; frozen shellfish can be bought very reasonably, and is fine for a barbecue. Serve with an arugula salad.

SERVES 4

8 wooden skewers
grated rind and juice of 2 limes
2 tbsp finely chopped lemon grass or 1 tbsp
    lemon juice
2 garlic cloves, crushed
1 green chili, deseeded and chopped
16 scallops, with corals
2 limes, each cut into 8 segments
2 tbsp sunflower oil
1 tbsp lemon juice
salt and pepper

TO SERVE:
1 cup arugula
3 cups mixed salad greens

1 Soak the skewers in warm water for at least 20 minutes before you use them.

2 Combine the lime juice and rind, lemon grass, garlic and chili together in a pestle and mortar or spice grinder to make a paste.

3 Thread 2 scallops onto each of the soaked skewers, alternating with 2 lime segments.

4 Whisk together the oil, lemon juice, salt and pepper thoroughly to make the salad dressing.

5 Coat the scallops with the spice paste, and place over a medium barbecue, basting occasionally.

6 Cook for 10 minutes, turning once.

7 Toss the arugula, mixed salad greens and dressing together well. Put into a serving bowl.

8 Serve the scallops piping hot, 2 skewers on each plate.

SALAD DRESSINGS

Make up salad dressings in screw-top glass jars. It is easy to see the proportions as you pour the oil and lemon juice or vinegar in. These should be 2 or 3 parts oil to 1 part acid. Add the remaining ingredients, screw the lid on tight, and shake well!

SEABASS BAKED IN FOIL

Seabass is often paired with subtle oriental flavors. For a special occasion, you may like to bone the fish, so that your guests cut straight through the flesh.

STEP 1

SERVES 4–6

2 seabass, about 2 pounds each, cleaned and scaled
2 scallions, green part only, cut into strips
2 garlic cloves, unpeeled, lightly crushed
2-in. piece gingerroot, peeled and cut into strips
2 tbsp mirin or dry sherry
salt and pepper

TO SERVE:
pickled sushi ginger (optional)
soy sauce

1 For each fish lay out a double thickness of foil, and oil the top piece well, or lay a piece of silicon paper over the foil.

2 Place the fish in the middle, and expose the cavity.

3 Divide the scallion and gingerroot between each cavity. Put a garlic clove in each cavity. Pour over the mirin. Season well.

4 Close the cavities, and lay each fish on its side.

5 Bring over the foil, and fold over the edges and ends to seal securely.

6 Cook over a medium barbecue for 15 minutes, turning once.

7 To serve, remove the foil, and cut each fish into 2 or 3 pieces. Serve with the pickled ginger, accompanied by soy sauce.

STEP 2

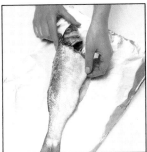

STEP 3

BONING THE FISH

To bone the fish, cover a chopping board with baking parchment, and lay the fish on it. Open up the cavity, and locate the rib bones. Insert a sharp vegetable knife under each bone on both sides of the backbone, and dislodge it from the flesh. Cut all these bones off with kitchen scissors. To remove the backbone, sever it near the tail, and as near to the head as possible. Open the fish out as wide as possible without tearing the flesh, and run the knife down either side of the spine, freeing the flesh from the backbone, but taking care not to cut through the skin. Remove the backbone. There will still be a few small bones.

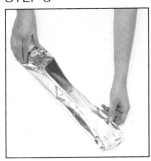

STEP 5

STEP 1

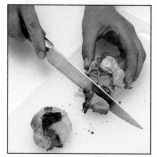

STEP 2

STEP 4

STEP 5

SWORDFISH STEAK WITH ROAST GARLIC

On a Saturday morning the fish market in Sydney is packed with people buying fish for their weekend "barbies", and swordfish is a very popular choice.

SERVES 4

4 swordfish steaks, about 7 ounces
  each
4 tbsp olive oil
2 whole garlic heads
pepper

1 Brush the swordfish steaks with the olive oil, and season well. Set aside.

2 Put the whole unpeeled garlic heads over a very hot barbecue, and cook for about 25 minutes until they are soft to the touch. It is difficult to overcook the garlic, but keep an eye on it nevertheless.

3 After the garlic has been cooking for about 15 minutes, put the steaks on the barbecue, and cook for 5–6 minutes on each side, until the flesh is firm and comes away from the bone easily. Brush once or twice with the olive oil during cooking.

4 When the garlic is soft to the touch, cut across the top of it, exposing all the cloves.

5 When the swordfish steaks are cooked, place on a serving plate, and squeeze the garlic straight out of the cloves across the top. Smear it all over liberally.

6 Season with pepper, and serve immediately.

GARLIC

When garlic is cooked like this, the sweetness of it comes to the fore. Although it does retain some of its pungency, it can be used more liberally than raw or slightly cooked garlic.

STEP 1

STEP 2

STEP 3

STEP 5

BABY OCTOPUS & SQUID WITH CHILI SAUCE

This is a delicious and unusual recipe, best served with a simple green salad. Try to buy cleaned squid tubes; if they are not available, see page 76 for instructions on preparing squid.

SERVES 4–6

²/₃ cup rice vinegar
¼ cup dry sherry
2 red chilies, chopped
1 tsp sugar
4 tbsp oil
12 baby octopus
12 small squid tubes, cleaned
2 scallions, sliced
1 garlic clove, crushed
1-in. piece gingerroot, grated
4 tbsp sweet chili sauce
salt

1 Combine the rice vinegar, sherry, red chilies, sugar, 2 tablespoons of the oil and a pinch of salt in a large bowl.

2 Wash each octopus under cold running water, and drain. Lay each on its side on a board. Find the "neck" and cut through. The "beak" of the octopus should be left in the head; if it is not, make a cut nearer the tentacles, and check again. Discard the head and beak, and put the tentacles, which should be in one piece, into the vinegar.

3 Put the squid tubes into the vinegar mixture. Cover and chill for 8 hours or overnight.

4 Put the remaining oil into a skillet or wok and add the scallions, garlic and gingerroot. Stir for 1 minute over a very hot barbecue. Remove from the heat, and add the chili sauce. Set aside.

5 Drain the fish from the marinade. Cut the pointed bottom end off each squid tube, so that you are left with tubes of even width all the way down. Make a cut down one side, and open out the squid so that it is flat. Make four cuts in one direction, and four in the other, taking care not to cut all the way through. You will have a lattice pattern.

6 Put all the octopus and squid over the hottest part of the barbecue for 4–5 minutes, turning them constantly. The octopus tentacles will curl up, and are cooked when the flesh is no longer translucent. The squid tubes will curl back on themselves, revealing the lattice cuts.

7 When cooked, toss them into the pan with the chili sauce to coat completely, and serve immediately.

CHAPTER THREE

Pork & Lamb

Fresh pork is grilled at a lower temperature than beef or lamb, as it needs to be cooked thoroughly, rather than be well done on the outside and raw in the middle. It is therefore possible that it may dry out when cooked. To prepare pork for the barbecue, wrap it in bacon, if in small pieces, or lard chops through the center with bacon fat. The pork satays here are cooked quickly in small pieces, so that they retain moisture. Ribs are traditionally crispy on the outside and succulent on the bone.

Lamb is the only meat that is suitable to cook in large cuts over a barbecue, as it retains its succulence. Even so, it does need attention in order to cook reasonably evenly and right through to the middle. A rôtisserie attachment will help with larger cuts, and enable you to cook these more evenly while you concentrate on the basting. Lamb is delicious barbecued, especially as it is so versatile. As well as the recipes included here, lamb can be cubed and skewered with bell peppers and onions, needing only seasoning and olive oil.

Both pork and lamb take on the flavors used in the marinade or for basting. Garlic, thyme, sage, parsley, chili, sesame oil, gingerroot, yogurt, mint and olive oil are all suitable for both meats.

Opposite: If you have room in your yard, a permanent brick-built barbecue is an excellent idea. It is sturdy and safe, and offers plenty of room for cooking up a feast.

STEP 1

STEP 2

STEP 3

STEP 4

PERSIAN LAMB

Chargrilling and lamb seem to be made for each other, and all over the Middle East both lamb and mutton are enjoyed in this way. The tabbouleh salad is a typical Middle Eastern accompaniment; if you are not keen on cilantro, substitute parsley.

SERVES 4–6

2 tbsp chopped fresh mint
1 cup natural yogurt
4 garlic cloves, crushed
$1/4$ tsp pepper
6 lamb chops
2 tbsp lemon juice

TABBOULEH:
2 cups couscous
2 cups boiling water
2 tbsp olive oil
2 tbsp lemon juice
$1/2$ onion, finely chopped
4 tomatoes, chopped
$1/2$ cup fresh cilantro, chopped
2 tbsp chopped fresh mint
salt and pepper

1 Combine the mint, yogurt, garlic and pepper.

2 Put the chops into a non-porous dish, and rub all over with the lemon juice. Pour over the yogurt marinade. Cover and marinate for 2–3 hours.

3 Meanwhile, make the tabbouleh. Put the couscous into a heatproof bowl, and pour over the boiling water.

Let steep for 5 minutes. Drain and put into a strainer. Set over a pan of barely simmering water, and steam for 8 minutes.

4 Toss in the oil and lemon juice. Add the onion, tomato, cilantro and mint. Season well, and set aside.

5 Cook the lamb over a medium barbecue for 15 minutes, turning once.

6 Serve with the tabbouleh.

YOGURT

Yogurt is a useful ingredient as a base for a marinade. The bland taste is a good medium for many flavors such as herbs, citrus fruit, spices and oils.

STEP 2

STEP 3

STEP 4

STEP 5

LAMB FILLET WITH ROASTED BABY ONIONS

This dish should be marinated overnight to tenderize the lamb. A long marinating also insures that the flavors seep into the meat, and keep it moist while cooking.

SERVES 6–8

1 pound lamb fillet
1 pound pearl onions
1 tbsp olive oil
3 tbsp chopped fresh thyme
2 lemons, rinsed and thickly sliced

MARINADE:
4 tbsp olive oil
3 garlic cloves, well crushed
$^{1}/_{2}$ tsp salt
$^{1}/_{2}$ tsp pepper

1 To make the marinade, mix the ingredients together to form a paste.

2 Smear the paste all over the lamb fillet, and let marinate overnight in the refrigerator.

3 Cook the onions in a saucepan of boiling water for about 15 minutes, until almost cooked through. Peel them.

4 Heat the oil and thyme in a skillet and add the onions to reheat them and coat them in the oil and thyme. Set aside.

5 Lay enough lemon slices over a very hot barbecue for the lamb to sit on.

6 Place the lamb on top, and cook for 10 minutes on each side, basting frequently.

7 Meanwhile, put the onions on the grid around the lamb, and cook for 10 minutes, turning often until they are quite soft but charred on the outside. Serve the lamb with the onions and a green bean salad.

HANDY HINT

The lamb should be hot all the way through, but still slightly pink and juicy in the center. However, if you prefer your lamb to be cooked for longer, barbecue it for 25 minutes. The marinade will keep the meat succulent.

KLEFTIKO

This classic Greek dish is usually made with leg of lamb. Here I have used a boneless leg. Serve with a classic Greek pilaf. Keep a close eye on the barbecue to insure the heat remains even during cooking.

STEP 1

SERVES 6–8

2-pound leg of lamb, boned and butterflied
6 tbsp olive oil
4 tbsp lemon juice
2 tbsp chopped fresh mint
$\frac{1}{2}$ tsp pepper
5 garlic cloves, sliced
2 fresh rosemary sprigs, broken into 20
    short lengths
$\frac{1}{2}$ onion, chopped
1 cup basmati rice
$1\frac{1}{4}$ cups chicken stock
1 tbsp pine nuts
1 tbsp chopped fresh oregano
2 eggplants, sliced lengthways
2 tbsp extra virgin olive oil
salt and pepper

1 Roll the lamb into a leg shape. Tuck in the shank (thin) end. Fasten in place with skewers, preferably metal.

2 Make 20 small nicks in the skin of the lamb with the tip of a knife.

3 Combine 4 tbsp of the olive oil with the lemon juice, mint, and pepper in a saucepan. Bring it to a slow boil. Pour the barely simmering marinade over the lamb, and rub in all over.

4 Insert a garlic slice and rosemary sprig into each nick. Place the lamb on a piece of double foil, or in a large foil tray, on the grid over a medium barbecue.

5 Cook the lamb for 15 minutes, turning frequently. Then turn every 10–15 minutes for about 1 hour, until the lamb is cooked through. You may need to change the foil during this time to avoid flare-ups. Because the lamb is an uneven shape, the shank end will be more well cooked than the large end.

6 Make the rice pilaf. Cook the onion and remaining olive oil in a saucepan over a low heat until the onion is softened, about 5 minutes. Add the rice, and stir until translucent. Add the stock and bring to a boil. Season well, and simmer over a low heat for 15 minutes. Stir in the pine nuts and oregano. Keep warm.

7 Cut a lattice pattern in the eggplant slices. Brush with the extra virgin olive oil, and cook on the grid for 10 minutes, turning once.

8 Slice the lamb, and serve with the eggplant and pilaf.

STEP 2

STEP 4

STEP 5

SWEET & SOUR PORK RIBS

Here I have used the sparerib, the traditional Chinese-style rib.
Baby back ribs and loin ribs are also suitable in this recipe.

STEP 1

STEP 2

STEP 4

STEP 5

SERVES 4–6

2 garlic cloves, crushed
2-in. piece gingerroot, grated
²/₃ cup soy sauce
2 tbsp sugar
4 tbsp sweet sherry
4 tbsp tomato paste
2 cups pineapple, cubed
4 pounds pork spareribs
3 tbsp clear honey
5 pineapple rings, fresh or canned

1 Combine the garlic, gingerroot, soy sauce, sugar, sherry, tomato paste and cubed pineapple in a non-porous dish.

2 Put the spareribs into the dish, and make sure that they are coated completely with the marinade. Cover the dish.

3 Leave at room temperature for 2 hours only.

4 Cook the ribs over a medium barbecue for 30–40 minutes, brushing with honey after 20–30 minutes. Baste with the reserved marinade frequently until cooked.

5 Cook the pineapple rings over the barbecue for 10 minutes, turning once.

6 Serve the ribs, with pineapple rings on the side.

MARINATING

If a marinade contains soy sauce, the marinating time should be limited, usually to 2 hours. If marinated for too long, the meat will dry out and become tough.

STEP 1

STEP 2

STEP 3

STEP 5

PORK SATAY

This is the classic satay, which can also be made with chicken. Here the slivers of pork make delicate skewers, which will cook quickly.

SERVES 6–8

36 wooden skewers, soaked in hand-hot
*   water for 20 minutes*
2 pounds pork (chump end or leg steaks)
1 small onion, finely sliced
2 garlic cloves, crushed
1 tsp ground coriander
1 tsp ground cumin
2 red chilies, deseeded and chopped
1-in. piece gingerroot, grated
2 tbsp soy sauce
2 tbsp oil
1 tbsp lemon juice
1 tsp dark brown sugar

PEANUT SAUCE:
1 small onion, quartered
3 garlic cloves, crushed
$\frac{1}{2}$ tsp ground coriander
$\frac{1}{2}$ tsp ground cumin
1 tbsp lemon juice
1 tsp salt
$\frac{1}{2}$ red chili, deseeded and sliced
$\frac{1}{2}$ cup coconut milk
1 cup crunchy peanut butter
1 cup water

1 Cut the pork into slivers, about 5 inches long and $\frac{1}{2}$ in. thick. Put into a non-porous dish.

2 Combine the onion, garlic, coriander, cumin, chilies, gingerroot, soy sauce, oil, lemon juice and brown sugar. Pour over the pork, and stir to make sure that it is evenly coated. Let marinate for 2–3 hours.

3 Meanwhile, make the peanut sauce. Chop the onion finely by hand, or feed it through the feed tube of a food processor. Then add the remaining ingredients in order, except for the water, and combine thoroughly.

4 Transfer to a saucepan, and add the water. Bring to a boil, and cook until the desired thickness is reached. Set aside.

5 Thread the pork slivers onto the soaked skewers in an "S" shape.

6 Cook over a medium barbecue for 10 minutes, turning frequently.

7 Serve hot or cold, accompanied by the peanut sauce.

STEP 1

STEP 2

STEP 3

STEP 6

SAUSAGES

It seems that no matter how many ribs, chicken wings or burgers go on the barbecue, the sausages always disappear first! So here is how to get a good result.

SERVES 4

4 barbecue pork sausages, the double-length
* kind, or 8 standard size sausages*
oil for brushing

TO SERVE:
1 onion
1 stick French bread, cut into 4
Dijon mustard

1 Prick the sausages all over with a fork. This not only insures that the skin does not split, but also lets the excess fat run out. Pork and beef sausages work very well on a barbecue, as they are quite firm.

2 Brush the sausages all over with oil – this also protects the skin.

3 Cook the sausages over a hot barbecue for 10 minutes, turning frequently. If you are using standard-sized pork sausages, they will cook in less time.

4 Cut the onion into 8 pieces, each piece held together by a bit of onion root. Brush with oil, and cook over the barbecue for 2–3 minutes.

5 Meanwhile, insert a bread knife through the inside of each piece of French bread. Without breaking the crust, hollow out enough bread for the sausage to fit in.

6 Spread a line of mustard through the middle of the bread. Put 2 pieces of onion in each piece, and push the cooked sausage through the middle. If using standard-sized sausages, put one in each end.

HANDY HINT

For an emergency barbecue recipe, defrost a packet of frozen sausages, and marinate them in a shop-bought marinade. Ready in minutes and guaranteed to be popular! There are several prepared marinades available; the best for sausages would be a spicy tomato-based one.

CHAPTER FOUR

Beef

Beef is a universally popular meat, and it tastes and smells superb when it is slowly cooked to perfection on top of a smouldering barbecue. Different countries treat it in different ways; in Texas, where thousands of cattle are reared every year, and where the butchers supply cuts of beef that aren't even available in many countries, it is eaten with an incomparable Texan barbecue sauce. It is enjoyed in Italy, usually as plainly cooked steak accompanied by a Barolo wine. In France several cuts are popular, such as fillet and Châteaubriand, but the rump skirt is the favorite for barbecues.

It is important to have the barbecue at the correct heat for the relevant cut of beef. A fillet must be cooked over a very high heat in order to retain moisture in this dry cut. Sirloin or rump has a higher fat content, and can have a longer cooking time. Rump would benefit from being marinated in an oil-based marinade. All steak cuts are improved by being barbecued in one piece, and sliced afterwards – again this retains moisture and flavor. Rump skirt must be cooked in one piece, as it is too grainy to be sliced first, and would lose its shape. The membranes must be removed so that the meat stays in shape while it cooks. Bearing these points in mind, beef is always the most popular meat at any barbecue, and, I find, the most satisfying to eat.

Opposite: *However ambitious your barbecue, it is unlikely to outshine this immense example, held in Buenos Aires, where the Argentinians make the most of their home-produced beef.*

STEP 1

STEP 2

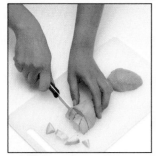

STEP 4

STEP 5

TEX-MEX RIBS

When you order your meat, ask for the ribs taken from between the 1st and 5th rib. If the ribs are quite fatty, cut off excess fat halfway through cooking, and return the lean meat to the grill.

SERVES 4–6

1 cup tomato ketchup
¼ cup cider vinegar
⅓ cup light muscovado sugar
1 onion, chopped
3 garlic cloves, crushed
1 tbsp dried chili flakes
2 tbsp Dijon mustard
1 tsp Worcestershire sauce
4 pounds prime beef ribs

TO SERVE:
1 stick French bread, sliced
½ cup butter
3 garlic cloves, crushed
1 tbsp chopped fresh parsley
1 avocado
lemon juice
4 cups mixed salad greens
salt and pepper

1 Combine the ketchup, vinegar, sugar, onion, garlic, chili flakes, mustard and Worcestershire sauce in a saucepan. Bring to a boil, and simmer for 10 minutes.

2 Wrap the ribs in foil, either in one piece or 3–4 smaller packages. Cook over a medium barbecue for 10 minutes, turning once or twice.

3 Meanwhile, place the sliced French bread in foil. Combine the butter, garlic and parsley with plenty of salt and pepper. Spread a little butter between each slice of the bread, and close the foil.

4 Peel and dice the avocado. Sprinkle over the lemon juice, and mix together with the salad greens.

5 Unwrap the ribs, and place over the hot barbecue. Baste with the ketchup mixture. Cook for 20 minutes, turning occasionally.

6 Cook the garlic bread alongside the ribs, for 15–20 minutes.

7 Serve the ribs piping hot, with any leftover barbecue sauce for dipping, the garlic bread and the green salad.

PERFECT TIMING

The ribs can be cooked over direct heat for their total cooking time, but precooking in the foil insures that the meat retains some moisture. To cook over direct heat, cook for 30 minutes, turning 3 or 4 times, and brushing with the barbecue sauce after 15 minutes. This will give a crusty finish.

PROVENCAL GRILLED BEEF

This recipe makes use of a coarse-grained but very tasty cut of beef called rump. You will find that it is very reasonably priced.

STEP 1

STEP 2

STEP 3

STEP 6

SERVES 6–8

2 pounds rump steak
$^1/_2$ tsp pepper
4 tbsp French olive oil
6 anchovies, finely chopped
2 garlic cloves, finely chopped
2 tbsp chopped fresh Italian parsley
2 tsp sea salt
French bread to serve

1 With a sharp knife, trim any excess fat from the meat. Pare off any membrane or connective tissue, which will misshape the meat as it cooks.

2 Rub in pepper and 1 tbsp of the olive oil all over the meat. Cover and chill for about 2 hours.

3 Combine the anchovies, garlic, parsley, sea salt, and remaining olive oil.

4 Remove the meat from the refrigerator 30 minutes before cooking.

5 Place the beef over a hot barbecue and cook for 8 minutes. Turn over, spread the anchovy mix on the top side, and cook for 6 minutes on the other side.

6 When the beef is cooked, remove to a chopping board. Let rest for 1 minute before slicing thinly.

7 Transfer to a warmed serving platter and serve with the French bread.

OLIVE OIL

In Italian homes seed oil is usually used for cooking, while the olive oil and extra virgin olive oil are used only as a table condiment. Extra virgin olive oil is a highly priced commodity, and has a delicate balance. Its structure and taste change upon heating, as well as its nutritional content; for this reason it should be used only as a dressing. Olive oil has a higher resilience to heat, being a coarser product, and is suitable for barbecuing and delicious for deep-frying. I have chosen French olive oil for this recipe as a personal preference, but Italian would do just as well.

STEAK IN A RED WINE MARINADE

The steak should be at least 1 in. thick, but not more than 3 inches thick. Fillet, sirloin, rump and porterhouse are all suitable, although I prefer rump, as it retains the most flavor.

STEP 1

SERVES 4

4 rump steaks, about 8 ounces each
2¹/₂ cups red wine
1 onion, quartered
2 tbsp Dijon mustard
2 garlic cloves, crushed
salt and pepper
4 large field mushrooms
olive oil for brushing
branch of fresh rosemary (optional)

1 Snip through the fat strip on the steaks in 3 places, so that the steak retains its shape when barbecued.

2 Combine the red wine, onion, mustard, garlic, salt and pepper. Lay the steaks in a shallow non-porous dish, and pour over the marinade. Cover and chill for 2–3 hours.

STEP 2

3 Remove the steaks from the refrigerator 30 minutes before you intend to cook them to let them come to room temperature. This is especially important if the steak is thick, so that it cooks more evenly, and is not well done on the outside and raw in the middle.

4 Sear both sides of the steak – about 1 minute on each side – over a hot barbecue. If it is about 1 in. thick, keep it over a hot barbecue, and cook for about 4 minutes on each side. This will give a medium-rare steak – cook it more or less, to suit your taste. If the steak is a thicker cut, move it to a less hot part of the barbecue, or farther away from the coals. To test the readiness of the meat while cooking, simply press it with your finger – the more the meat yields, the less it is cooked.

STEP 4

5 Brush the mushrooms with the olive oil, and cook them alongside the steak, for 5 minutes, turning once. When you put the mushrooms on the barbecue, put the rosemary branch in the fire to flavor the meat slightly.

6 Remove the steak, and let rest for a minute or two before serving. Slice the mushrooms, and serve alongside.

COOKING TIMES

Cooking times are variable. A tender fillet will take a much shorter time than a rump or T-bone steak, so the best judge will be your own eye. Test the steaks frequently for readiness, according to taste.

STEP 5

STEP 1

STEP 2

STEP 2

STEP 4

BEEF PATTIES

The traditional beefburger needs no egg to hold it together. Flavorings can be added, and a combination of meats used. Do not be tempted to use extra-lean ground meat as the result will be too dry; any excess fat will drain off anyway.

SERVES 4

2 cups ground beef
1 cup ground lamb
1 onion, finely chopped
6 tomatoes, halved
1 red onion, finely chopped
1 red chili, deseeded and chopped
2 tbsp dark brown sugar
$^{1}/_{4}$ cup cider vinegar
1 tsp balsamic or sherry vinegar
2 tbsp chopped fresh chervil (optional)
4 soft hamburger rolls
$^{1}/_{2}$ iceberg lettuce, shredded
4 gherkins
mustard
salt and pepper

1 Combine the beef, lamb and onion in a large bowl with plenty of salt and pepper.

2 It is important that the patties do not have any air pockets. To insure this, divide the mixture into 4, and make 1 ball from each quarter. Put each ball in a cupped hand, and throw it into the other hand to compact the mixture, repeating a few times until you have a dense ball of meat. Put this on a plate, and press gently with the palm of your hand to make the ball into a patty. Chill.

3 Put the tomato halves on a rack over a baking sheet. Bake in a preheated oven at 350°F for 40–50 minutes until quite collapsed.

4 Chop the tomato coarsely, and combine with the red onion, red chili, sugar and vinegars. Season well, and add chervil, if using. Transfer to a serving dish, and set aside.

5 Cook the patties over a hot barbecue for 10 minutes, turning once. This will give a medium-rare burger – for a well-done burger, cook for 15 minutes. Toward the end of cooking time, split the soft rolls, and toast lightly for 1–2 minutes on the cut side.

6 Put some shredded lettuce, the beefburger, a gherkin and mustard to taste on the bottom half of the toasted roll, and cover with the top half. Serve with the salsa.

HANDY HINT

The best size for a beef patty is a 3-in. round. Compact the mixture well, and chill thoroughly to insure the patty keeps in shape when it is cooked.

PAN BAGNA

This is a deliciously moist picnic dish, lunch dish or anytime snack. It is of Italian origin, designed for workers to take to the fields in a box.

STEP 1

STEP 3

STEP 4

STEP 5

SERVES 4

1 red bell pepper, halved, cored and deseeded
8-ounce sirloin steak, 1 in. thick
1 small white oblong loaf or stick French
    bread
4 tbsp olive oil
2 extra-large tomatoes, sliced
10 black olives, halved
½ English cucumber, peeled and sliced
6 anchovies, chopped
salt and pepper

1 Cook the bell pepper over a hot barbecue for 15 minutes, turning once. Put it into a plastic bag, and seal the bag.

2 Sear both sides of the steak first, and then grill for 8 minutes, turning once.

3 When the bell pepper is cool enough to handle, peel and slice it. Cut the steak into thin strips.

4 Cut the bread lengthways, and hollow out each half, leaving a 1-in. crust. Brush both halves very liberally with olive oil.

5 Lay the tomatoes, olives, cucumber, steak strips, anchovies and red bell pepper strips on the bottom half. Season and cover with the top half.

6 Put the Pan Bagna on top of a piece of baking parchment. Squash the whole loaf and its filling down well, and wrap tightly in plastic wrap. Secure with adhesive tape if necessary. Chill for at least 2 hours. If made in the morning, by lunchtime it will be ready to eat, and all the flavors will have combined.

VARIATIONS

Different fillings, such as pâtés, sausages and other salad items, can be used according to appetite and taste. Mozzarella cheese is good, as it is so moist. Onions give a bit of a zing to the other ingredients.

FAJITAS

This is an ideal party dish, as all the constituents of the fajitas can be set out on a buffet for guests to construct themselves.

STEP 1

STEP 2

STEP 3

STEP 4

SERVES 4

4 tbsp corn oil
4 tbsp lime juice
2 tbsp chopped fresh cilantro
2 garlic cloves, crushed
1 tbsp chili flakes
1 pound top sirloin steak
4 flour tortillas
1 avocado, peeled, halved, pitted and sliced
$^1/_2$ iceberg lettuce, shredded
salt and pepper

SALSA:
2 plum tomatoes, deseeded and finely
    chopped
$^1/_4$ red onion, finely chopped
1 tbsp chopped fresh cilantro
2 tsp sunflower oil
1 tsp white wine vinegar
1 green chili, deseeded and finely chopped

1 Combine the corn oil, lime juice, cilantro, garlic, chili flakes, salt and pepper in a large non-porous dish.

2 Add the meat to this mixture, and make sure that it is coated all over.

3 Cover and marinate in the refrigerator for 8 hours or overnight.

4 Next day, combine the salsa ingredients, and transfer to a serving dish.

5 Cook the meat over a hot barbecue for 10–15 minutes, turning once. It should be slightly pink in the middle, and not completely firm when pressed. The time will depend on the thickness of the meat.

6 Remove from the grill, and slice thinly, across the grain. Divide between the 4 tortillas, alternating with the avocado slices, and putting a little shredded lettuce into each one. Wrap the tortilla around the filling.

7 Serve immediately, with the salsa and any other desired accompaniments. Serve with a cold Mexican beer, if liked.

CHAPTER FIVE

Vegetables

There are occasions when you will want to provide more than a cold salad buffet with your barbecues. At certain times of the year it is pleasant to have hot vegetables available, as well as, or instead of, cold salads. Most vegetables will have to be blanched before being barbecued to ensure they cook quickly and evenly. Some vegetables lend themselves very well to chargrilling, and I have given recipes for those that I think are the best accompaniments to the other dishes in this book.

However, other vegetables can also be barbecued – carrots, scallions, mushrooms and pumpkin all sweeten up over the charcoal. Many vegetables, such as pumpkin, potatoes and eggplants, can be cooked in large pieces in foil over the barbecue. Whole onions can be cooked in the embers – simply slice off both ends, leave the skin on, and nestle them in the embers for 45 minutes; they soften up and become deliciously sweet, and can be eaten on their own, or served on top of other food, such as sausages and burgers.

Opposite: *Most vegetables take on a sweet, smoky flavor when barbecued, and it is worth experimenting with a wide range to find your favorite.*

STEP 1

STEP 2

STEP 3

STEP 4

STUFFED RED BELL PEPPERS

Stuffed bell peppers are a well-known dish, but this is a new version adapted for the barbecue. The roasted vegetables create a tasty Mediterranean vegetable dish.

SERVES 4

2 red bell peppers, halved lengthways and
　deseeded
2 tomatoes, halved
2 zucchini, thinly sliced lengthways
1 red onion, cut into 8 sections, each section
　held together by the root
4 tbsp olive oil
2 tbsp fresh thyme leaves
1/3 cup mixed basmati and wild rice, cooked
salt and pepper

1 Put the halved bell peppers, halved tomatoes, sliced zucchini and onion sections onto a baking sheet.

2 Brush the vegetables with olive oil, and sprinkle over the thyme leaves.

3 Cook the bell pepper, onion and zucchini over a medium barbecue for 6 minutes, turning once.

4 When the bell peppers are cooked, put a spoonful of the cooked rice into each one, and the onion and zucchini on top.

5 Cook the tomato halves for 2–3 minutes only, before adding a half to each stuffed bell pepper.

6 Season with plenty of salt and pepper, and serve.

BELL PEPPERS

When chargrilled, red, orange and yellow bell peppers all take on a remarkable sweet quality. They are often peeled in order to highlight this. Orange bell peppers are worth experimenting with as they do have a different flavor from red and green bell peppers. Both red and orange bell peppers complement lamb beautifully, and rice is a good foil to both of these. Try this dish with Lamb Fillet with Roasted Baby Onions (page 38), or Persian Lamb (page 36).

CORN-ON-THE-COB

Corn-on-the-cob is available nearly all the year round, and it can be barbecued with the husk on or off.

STEP 1

STEP 2

STEP 3

STEP 4

SERVES 4–6

4–6 corn-on-the-cobs
oil for brushing

TO SERVE:
butter (optional)
salt (optional)

1 Soak the cobs in hand-hot water for 20 minutes. Drain them thoroughly.

2 If the cobs have no green leaves, brush with oil, and cook over a hot barbecue for 30 minutes, brushing occasionally with the oil, and turning often.

3 If the cobs have green leaves, tear off all but the last two layers, and brush with oil.

4 Cook over a hot barbecue for 40 minutes, brushing with oil once or twice, and turning occasionally.

5 Serve hot, without the husks. If you like, add a small piece of butter, and salt to taste.

TIPS

Try to buy the cobs with the husk still on, as they will retain more moisture when barbecued this way.

Corn-on-the-cob is an excellent accompaniment to any American- or South American-style dish such as Blackened Chicken (page 16), Beef Patties (page 56) and Tex-Mex Ribs (page 50).

While you are barbecuing the corn-on-the-cob, you may like to flavor it with oils or herbs. Try tucking some rosemary, cilantro or thyme inside the husk for a deliciously aromatic flavor. A wide variety of herb oils and flavored oils can be bought – my favorite is hazelnut oil, which really adds something to corn-on-the-cob. You may also like to try a chili oil, or any of the oils that are flavored with herbs such as rosemary, thyme or basil.

ROASTED RED BELL PEPPER TERRINE

After cooking a delicious meal over the barbecue on a Saturday evening, roast some vegetables in order to make this delicious terrine for Sunday lunch. This goes well with Italian bread and a green salad.

STEP 1

STEP 6

STEP 7

STEP 8

SERVES 6–8

olive oil, to oil the terrine
3 cups fava beans
6 red bell peppers, halved, cored and deseeded
3 small zucchini, sliced lengthways
1 eggplant, sliced lengthways
3 leeks, halved lengthways
6 tbsp olive oil
6 tbsp light cream
2 tbsp chopped fresh basil
salt and pepper

1 Oil a 5-cup terrine. Blanch the fava beans in boiling water for 1–2 minutes, and pop them out of their skins. It is not essential to do this, but the effort is worthwhile as the beans taste a lot sweeter.

2 Roast the red bell peppers over a hot barbecue until the skin is black – about 10–15 minutes. Remove and put into a plastic bag. Seal and set aside.

3 Brush the zucchini, eggplant, and leeks with 5 tbsp of the olive oil, and season well. Cook over the hot barbecue until tender, about 8–10 minutes, turning once.

4 Meanwhile, purée the fava beans in a blender or food processor with 1 tablespoon of the olive oil, the cream, and seasoning. Alternatively, chop and then press through a strainer.

5 Remove the red bell peppers from the bag, and peel.

6 Put a layer of red bell pepper along the bottom and up the sides of the terrine.

7 Spread a third of the bean purée over this. Cover with the eggplant slices, and spread half of the remaining bean purée over the top.

8 Sprinkle over the basil. Top with zucchini and the remaining bean purée. Lay the leeks on top. Add any remaining pieces of red bell pepper. Put a piece of foil, folded 4 times, on the top and weigh down with cans.

9 Chill until required. Invert on a serving platter. Slice and serve with Italian bread and a green salad.

DEVILED NEW POTATOES

This is a way of giving potatoes, or any other root vegetable you have to hand, the star treatment. A barbecue needs smaller things like this to keep your diners happy while they wait for the main event.

STEP 2

SERVES 6–8

20 toothpicks
1 pound baby new potatoes
olive oil for brushing
10 slices bacon
20 small sage leaves

1 Soak the toothpicks in hand-hot water for 20 minutes before using.

2 Bring a pan of water to a boil, and add the potatoes. Boil for 10 minutes, and drain.

3 Brush the potatoes all over with olive oil.

4 Cut each bacon slice in half widthways. Holding each piece at one end, smooth and stretch it with the back of a knife.

5 Wrap a piece of bacon around each potato, enclosing a sage leaf and securing with a toothpick.

6 Cook over a hot barbecue for 6–7 minutes, turning occasionally. Serve hot or cold.

STEP 3

VARIATIONS

Either unsmoked or smoked bacon may be used to wrap the vegetables. I favor the smoked variety as it tends to keep its shape for longer than green bacon.

All manner of root vegetables can be wrapped in bacon, and grilled this way. Baby onions (the pickling variety) are especially delicious, as the outside skin turns crispy, golden and sweet. Carrots, parsnips and turnips will all need peeling and cutting down to 1-in. cubes, unless you make use of the baby varieties of these vegetables, in which case you need not peel them.

Any variety of pumpkin or squash should be peeled, deseeded and cut down to 1-in. cubes. The pumpkin family of vegetables turns remarkably sweet when heated. The same recipe can be used to cook leeks as well – peel and parboil as in the recipe, cut into 1-in. cubes, wrap in bacon and tuck in the sage leaf.

STEP 4

STEP 5

ROAST LEEKS

Use a good-quality French or Italian olive oil for this deliciously simple yet sophisticated vegetable accompaniment.

STEP 1

STEP 2

STEP 3

STEP 4

SERVES 4–6

4 leeks
3 tbsp olive oil
2 tsp balsamic vinegar
sea salt and pepper

1 Halve the leeks lengthways, making sure that your knife goes straight, so that the leek is held together by the root.

2 Brush each leek liberally with the olive oil.

3 Cook the leeks over a hot barbecue for 6–7 minutes, turning once.

4 Remove from the barbecue, and brush with the balsamic vinegar.

5 Sprinkle with salt and pepper, and serve hot or warm.

SEA SALT

Sea salt or *gros sel* (bay salt in some older cookery books) is a very inexpensive ingredient that will add another dimension to your dishes. It is made by panning on salt marshes near the coast and contains more magnesium and calcium than other salts. When scattered over a simple dish such as these leeks, it will bring out all the flavors, and will look attractive too, crumbled between the fingertips. Because of the sharp taste you will not need to use as much sea salt as you would rock salt.

SUBSTITUTES

If in season 8 baby leeks may be used instead of 4 regular-sized ones. Sherry vinegar makes a good substitute for the expensive balsamic vinegar, and would work as well in this recipe.

STEP 1

STEP 4

STEP 5

STEP 6

ROASTED VEGETABLES ON ROSEMARY SKEWERS

Rosemary branches can be used as brushes for basting and as skewers. If you buy them in a pack, look for the longest sprigs, though the best way to get long sprigs is, of course, to cut them from a bush.

SERVES 6

1 small red cabbage
1 head fennel
1 orange bell pepper, cut into 1¹/₂-in. dice
1 eggplant, halved and sliced into ¹/₂-in.
  pieces
2 zucchini, thickly sliced diagonally
olive oil for brushing
6 rosemary twigs, about 6 ins long, soaked
  for 8 hours or overnight in water
salt and pepper

1 Put the red cabbage on its side on a chopping board, and cut through the middle of its stem and heart. Divide each piece into 4, each time including a bit of the stem in the slice in order to hold it together.

2 Prepare the fennel in the same way.

3 Blanch the red cabbage and fennel in boiling water for 3 minutes, then drain well.

4 With a wooden skewer, pierce a hole through the middle of each piece of vegetable.

5 Onto each rosemary twig, thread a piece of orange bell pepper, fennel, red cabbage, eggplant and zucchini, pushing the rosemary through the holes.

6 Brush liberally with olive oil, and season with plenty of salt and pepper.

7 Cook over a hot barbecue for 8–10 minutes, turning occasionally. Serve hot.

FRUIT SKEWERS

Fruit skewers are a deliciously quick and easy dessert. Thread pieces of banana, mango, peach, strawberry, apple and pear onto soaked wooden skewers, and cook over the dying embers. Brush with sugar syrup toward the end of cooking.

SUCCESSFUL BARBECUING

Kachumber
2 tomatoes, chopped
$^1/_2$ red onion, sliced
$^1/_2$ English cucumber, chopped

Combine the tomatoes, onion, and cucumber at least 1 hour before serving in order to let the flavors mingle. Sprinkle with a little salt and toss together. Transfer to a serving dish.

Raita
$^2/_3$ cup natural yogurt
1 tsp chopped fresh mint
5 tbsp peeled and finely
    chopped English cucumber

Combine the yogurt, mint and cucumber. Season well with salt, and toss together. Transfer to a serving dish.

Preparing squid
To clean squid, put them all in a large sink full of cold water. Find the translucent backbone of each squid, and put your hand down between this and the flesh. When you find the bottom, pull it out in one piece with the head and tentacles, and discard. Scrape around the inside of the tube until it is clean. Rinse with cold water. Remove one of the wings from the tube, and then it will be easy to remove the dark skin and the other wing. Rinse again.

BARBECUES
For centuries people have built fires and cooked food over the flames or in the embers. Even though it is no longer necessary for most people to cook in this fashion, it remains an enjoyable way to cook, producing succulent food with an incomparable flavor. Barbecuing now takes slightly different forms all around the world, but the principles remain the same. In Australia and New Zealand the fire is in a pit; in the Middle East lamb is spit-roasted over white-hot embers. In the Mediterranean countries fish is grilled over an open wood fire on the beach, while a charcoal burner is fired up in Greece. A terracotta burner is also used in India, but it is sunk into the ground and known as a tandoor. And finally, we Americans adapted gas to use as a cooking fuel for barbecues, and created the quick and easy barbecue that many people use today.

The word "barbecue" comes from the Spanish *barbacoa*, which describes the process of grilling meat over an open wood fire on bars of wet green wood. Today it has also come to mean the cooking apparatus, and the social gathering at which food is barbecued.

TYPES OF BARBECUE
There are many types of barbecue to choose from, and you should consider a number of things before you decide which to buy or build. As the life of any barbecue will be shortened if it is left outside for the winter months, you will need some storage space, not to mention enough space to use the barbecue easily. Another factor is the number of people you cook for regularly – it is easier to cook for small numbers on a large barbecue than vice versa. The safety factor must be considered – if you have young children, you may not want to use hot charcoal, and the height of the grill will have to be considered too. The following types of barbecue are commonly available:

Disposable
Sturdy foil trays enclose a rack and enough charcoal to cook a meal for two people; ideal for the beach and also for where space is limited, such as on balconies. Be sure to put them on a heatproof surface – for example, a concrete floor or sand.

Hibachi-type
Japanese in origin, they are made of cast iron, and stand on four legs. They have air vents in the front to control the heat, and different height settings for the racks. They are ideal for cooking for one or two.

Charcoal burners
These are small free-standing, attractive round terracotta structures. They have air holes in the sides and a grid over the charcoal. They are rather small, but ideal for one or two people, and quite cheap.

Portable gas or charcoal
These are either floor-standing or

tabletop and are designed for camping trips or larger picnic parties. Some models are better than others, and features to look for are adjustable air vents and rack height. They are also ideal for barbecue cooking at home if you have only limited storage space.

Kettle barbecues

The purpose of covering the food as you cook it is to get a more even finish – especially important for large cuts of meat. Some kettle barbecues have a water tray above the coals in order to semi-steam the meat; this retains a lot of moisture and avoids shrinkage. I once ate a turkey cooked in a kettle barbecue, and it tasted marvelously moist.

Counter height

This is one of the most popular types of barbecue, and a wide selection of models is available with a range of extras. Your choice of the latter depends on for what and how often you intend to use the barbecue. Again, make a priority of adjustable rack height and air vents. There are other options that are not essential, but which tend to become indispensable once you have them, such as a work table, warming rack, rôtisserie, lid with viewing window, wheels, ash drainer, and adjustable temperature settings. This type of barbecue is the most sturdy, and ideal for families with children.

Brick-built

They can be built in many different sizes on ground level, slightly raised, or at counter height. The deluxe version is often seen clad in a decorative finish to match the surroundings, and with a built-in chimney to take the smoke away. The solid iron grid is quite large – around 40 × 24 inches.

Oil drums

These are very useful for large parties. The drum is cut in half lengthways, and supported on a metal construction or bricks. Air holes must be drilled along the side – at regular 4-in. intervals, I suggest. The charcoal is piled inside on top of lava rocks or stones, and the grid rested across the top of the drum.

FUELS

Once you have selected a barbecue, you have to decide the kind of fuel you wish to use, unless you can link up to natural gas, or plug in an electric "barbecue." Your choices are:

Portable gas

Butane is widely available, but some people believe that propane burns hotter. A European barbecue often cannot be used in America, as the available fuels are different.

Wood

Dried-out hardwoods are the best, as softwoods tend to impart resin flavors to the food. Fruit woods give a very nice flavor, as do olive woods and vines. Hickory chips and mesquite chips are natural wood products that are used alongside other fuels to flavor the food. Mesquite is very strong, and is usually used to "smoke" food as opposed to flaming it.

Preparing a chicken
To cut a chicken into 6 pieces, first insure that the chicken is quite cold, and that your chopping knife is really sharp. Set the chicken on one side, and hold the thigh and drumstick in one hand. Cut under the leg to the joint at the body, turn back the leg, and cut through the joint. Repeat with the other side. Set the chicken on its back with the breast uppermost and the wings toward you. Cut through the breast, about 1 in. away from the winglet, in a straight line downward. You should be left with the wing attached to a bit of breast meat. Repeat with the other winglet. Make an initial incision along one side of the breastbone to detach the breast from the bone. Cut around the edge of the breast, insuring that no flesh is left behind. Cut the breast carefully away from the bird. Repeat with the other breast.

Cheese
Hard cheeses, such as feta and Greek halloumi, are particularly suitable for barbecuing. Brie and Camembert can be flashed over the grill, and goat cheese is particularly delicious grilled quickly in whole "banons" or sliced and grilled on slices of bread.

Sweet treats

Marshmallows are a popular barbecue finale. Stick one on the end of a metal skewer or soaked wooden skewer, and hold over the hottest part of the barbecue for a maximum of 1 minute, after which they will drip off the stick. Eat with care – they are very hot when first removed from the flame.

Other post-barbecue treats include bananas in their skins tossed onto the dying fire and cooked for 15–30 minutes. When you peel off the skin, the banana falls out, as if it were relieved to be out of the heat!

Pineapple can be cubed and skewered to be grilled, while apples and pears can be wrapped in foil and cooked slowly – delicious with whipped cream! Try putting a piece of fudge into the cored apple before baking in foil.

There are all kinds of things which seem to find their natural home at a barbecue patio party. A favorite of mine is to prepare a variety of fruits – melon, pineapple, kiwi, strawberries – peeled and cut into bite-sized pieces. Arrange on a couple of large plates with toothpicks to make them into finger food.

Charcoal

In the absence of wood this is the most popular fuel. Natural charcoal needs a bit of care in constructing the fire. Break up the large unmanageable pieces, and put the smaller pieces at the bottom and larger ones on top, insuring there is plenty of air circulation all around, and that it comes to the right height. Light it according to your preferred method (see below).

Charcoal briquettes

These are a convenient form of charcoal, but the quality varies. An artificial resin is used to compact the briquettes, and in some brands it is stronger than others. Try a few brands to discover the one that gives the best flavor to the food.

Charcoal bags

These are quite a modern invention, and have charcoal inside, which I find better than briquettes. A pack contains two 2-pound paper bags. The paper bag of charcoal is simply placed in the barbecue, and a match is set to it. The paper acts as kindling to stoke the fire.

Lava rocks

As these are the molten matter that flows from a volcano, they have an extremely high melting point. When heated, they will retain and radiate that heat, and are useful if used in conjunction with charcoal. Gas barbecues and indoor chargrills often use these to supply a little genuine flavor.

LIGHTING THE BARBECUE

All fires need oxygen to enable them to burn, and barbecues are no exception, so make sure that the air vents are working properly, and that the structure has plenty of air circulation, and you will be well on your way to a blazing barbecue.

The tried and tested method of lighting it is to put kindling – tightly rolled and knotted paper is a good substitute – underneath the charcoal. Starter fluid or firelighters can be used, but these do tend to leave a chemical flavor, however long they are left to burn – they are, however, the most convenient and cleanest to use.

A blowtorch is a useful gadget to have at this point, but must be used with great care. Heat can be applied to the base of the fire which will permeate throughout the coals without leaving any unwanted aromas.

Another useful gadget to have is a hand-held battery-operated fan – the kind that one uses in the summer to cool down – as this can push air through the fire to oxygenate it, and increase the heat. The barbecue is ready when the embers are white hot, or the charcoal is covered in a fine white-gray ash.

Always have extra fuel on standby to stoke the fire, and do as much advance preparation on the food as possible, as the barbecue will need regular tending in order to get the best, most constant heat from it.

If you are using a larger barbecue than you need, insure the fire covers an area at least 2 inches larger than the food.

Levels of heat

I have specified the different levels of heat needed for different foods throughout the recipes. These levels can be measured by

holding your hand over the barbecue, about 6 inches away from the coals. If you can bear to hold it there
 – for 4 seconds, the heat is low-medium
 – for 3 seconds, the heat is medium
 – for 2 seconds, the heat is high
 – for 1 second, the heat is very high
The heat can be adjusted by raising or lowering the rack. I find that a pair of charcoal tongs is useful for tending the barbecue – special charcoal tongs can be bought, but a pair of standard metal tongs is sufficient, as long as the tongs are reserved for this purpose.

TOOLS
Other tools that you may find useful – in order of necessity – are:

Metal tongs
Preferably long-handled, for turning the food over. They do not pierce flesh and thus drain juices as a fork would.

Gloves
Heavy-duty gardening gloves or welders' gloves are best, both for picking up baked potatoes and for building the fire.

Work table
A small work table is most useful for storing equipment and ingredients.

Apron
A plastic wipe-clean apron is ideal.

Basting brush
To keep everything moist while cooking.

Water pistol
This is the easiest thing to use to extinguish or prevent flare-ups. However, this should *not* be used on electric barbecues in any circumstances, nor on gas barbecues, as you might extinguish the gas flames, leaving the gas seeping out without burning.

Wire brush
To brush down the barbecue after use. It is essential to start cooking with a clean rack, so that the meat does not stick.

Long fork
Useful to turn things, and used together with the tongs to turn large cuts of meat.

Warming rack
This is a useful addition while waiting for everything else to finish cooking.

Rôtisserie
Not essential, but it does make cooking larger cuts of meat a great deal easier.

Potato rack
Four spikes arranged in a round conduct heat through the potato, and cook it quickly. A skewer is a good substitute.

Skewers
Metal skewers are best, All sorts of food can be skewered and cooked with only a little basting needed. Wooden skewers can be used, but need to be soaked in water first to prevent them from burning.

Rib rack, fuel holder, ash drainer, and grill baskets
These and many other extras are available. None of them is essential, but can be useful if you barbecue often.

SAMPLE MENUS

*For a large informal party
of 20 or more:*

Pork Satay
Sausage
Fajitas
Corn-on-the-cob
Roasted Vegetables on
   Rosemary Skewers

Fruit salad
or
Fruit Pavlova

*For a formal barbecue
for 4–8 people:*

Scallop Skewers

Tasmanian Duck
Roast Leeks
Deviled New Potatoes
Green salad

Cheese

*For a family get-together
of 12 or more:*

Chargrilled Chicken Salad

Salmon Fillet on a Bed of Herbs
Beef Patties
Green salad
Baked potatoes
Stuffed Red Bell Peppers

Ice cream
Fruit salad

INDEX